BY THE HAND OF GOD

by

Wendi Landis-Talkington

DORRANCE
PUBLISHING CO
EST. 1920
PITTSBURGH, PENNSYLVANIA 15238

The contents of this work, including, but not limited to, the accuracy of events, people, and places depicted; opinions expressed; permission to use previously published materials included; and any advice given or actions advocated are solely the responsibility of the author, who assumes all liability for said work and indemnifies the publisher against any claims stemming from publication of the work.

Dorrance Publishing Co
585 Alpha Drive
Suite 103
Pittsburgh, PA 15238
Visit our website at *www.dorrancebookstore.com*

ISBN: 978-1-6453-0243-8
eISBN: 978-1-6453-0772-3

INSPIRATIONAL NOTE

This a true story about how a serious illness can affect a family and how faith and prayer can bring life back into your soul. It's for the family that donated their loved one's organ, so that I might live. It's to all you readers that are on a transplant list to know that there is life after transplant. This book is dedicated to all those people around the world that prayed for me. It's to my family and friends who saw me in my darkest hours and prayed at my bedside. It's for my children who are the biggest blessing I could have ever received. This is to all of you readers that I might bring God into your heart that you will feel his spirit as I do. Don't let any struggles, that you have, define who you are. Don't give up no matter what curve ball you are given. Be happy and live your life, because it is yours to live.

QUESTION IN TIME

Have you ever been in a situation where life is just not going right? Everything just seems to fall apart? Did you ever question if there was a God? Do you hear stories that you just don't believe or that you don't want to believe the stories because they seem so off the wall that they can't be true? I think I will start off telling you some feelings that I had and what made me have them.

At the time when my life started to take a bad turn, I was thirty-five years old and my children were sixteen, ten, and six. My husband, at the time, and I had been having problems for quite some time. There were many arguments and loud voices and we had just basically grown apart as time went on.

I loved my husband, but I just did not feel that love in return. He spent a lot of time with his friends and not that much time with his family. Now I wasn't a regular at church, but I did believe in saying my prayers nightly. As my frustration grew with my relationship with my husband, I would turn to prayer to try and make a plea for help. I often asked God to make it better, but there were no changes in the relationship. It seemed like it only got worse. On one night, I was so desperate that I asked God to let something happen to me so that my husband would feel love for me and would know that he needed me in his life. As I lay in bed crying, I asked myself, "How do I know there is a God? There is no proof so maybe the Bible is just a story." That is when my life took a dramatic change and I was about to learn my lesson.

THANKSGIVING

About two weeks after that prayer, if even that long, I went to the doctor with a bladder infection. This was on the Wednesday before Thanksgiving in 2000. The nurse practitioner saw me and did some blood work and checked my vitals. The doctor was really busy that day, so I wasn't able to see him. The nurse said that my white blood count was low. She confirmed that I did have a bladder infection, so she gave me a shot of Rocephin and some Keflex pills, which are in the same family as Rocephin. She then scheduled a follow up appointment for Friday the day after Thanksgiving.

I was a full-time working mother and kept a busy schedule with my four children. I was a JV cheerleading coach at my daughter's high school. As all mothers know, there is no time for sickness when we have children at home. So as a mother, you keep pushing on even when you feel lousy.

The Wednesday before Thanksgiving there was always a high school basketball game. I was feeling terrible by late in the afternoon, so I called the varsity coach to let her know that I would not be able to make the game. As the evening progressed, I began to feel like something was seriously wrong. My body was covered in sweat because my fever had reached 104, and I had a rash covering my body. I did not want to call the doctor at such late hours, so I waited until 6:00 a.m. on Thanksgiving morning. When I spoke with the nurse on call, she told me it sounded like an allergic reaction to the antibiotic. The nurse said to send my husband to the store to get Benadryl. She said if it did not get any better in a few hours to go to the emergency room.

Since it was Thanksgiving, we had company from out of town come up for the holiday. We had a big dinner planned at my parents' house. At this point, I was so disoriented from the fever, I called my mother to come and get the children so that my husband could take me to the emergency room. My children were reluctant to leave, but I gave them hugs and kisses and reassured them that I would be over to Grandma's and Grandpa's house as soon as I was done at the hospital. I told them to save me some turkey and with some hesitation, they smiled and left.

When I got to the emergency room, I told them what the nurse on call had said. She had thought I was having an allergic reaction to the antibiotic, Rocephin. A nurse took me back to a check in room and took my blood pressure and found it was very low. The rash was obvious and severe at that point. My temperature was still at 104 degrees. They did a urine analysis and my urine was dark orange. At that point, the doctors said they were not going to let me go home and they were going to keep me a few days under observation. They said something was going on with me and they needed to run some further tests to figure out the cause of what was going on. That's when my life took a drastic turn. They hooked me up to an IV antibiotic and sent me up to a room where I progressively got worse. I started to produce blisters ranging in different sizes all over my body. They were growing and filling with fluid right before my eyes. My fever started to rise and spiked to 107. They tried to get my temperature down by packing me with ice. I could hear conversations, but I could not really comprehend what was being said due to my fever and shivering from the ice. I do remember hearing a nurse say, "please don't die on my watch." Then it hit me, and I was terrified! Was I really that sick? I have never been sick. I was not sure what was going on. I was disoriented. I couldn't move because of the blisters that were now covering eighty percent of my body. My blood pressure was extremely low, and I was weak.

THE DIAGNOSIS

The next morning, I looked up and saw that they were giving me Rocephin intravenously, I panicked, and I told the nurse to change the antibiotic because the Rocephin was killing me. The nurse said to me, "That's what the doctor ordered, that's what you're going to get." Words that I will never forget for the rest of my life. When the doctor came in that morning, I asked why was I on that medicine? and he told me that he wasn't convinced that the medicine was causing the illness. He thought I might have small pox, measles, or the Ebola virus. I told him, I think it is the antibiotic. He said it was too mild of an antibiotic and he felt strongly that it was something else. I started to panic. The doctor and nurses that I trusted my life with were totally and completely oblivious to what I was telling them. In fact, they were killing me. As that day went on, my condition was getting worse. The hospital called doctors in from all over to find a diagnosis. I was being tested for different viruses and illness. They would put me in isolation and then remove me from isolation. I was in a state of complete and utter frustration! Why could they not figure out what was going on? Finally, a lady doctor from California came into to my room. She had heard of my condition and she looked at me and said, "Stop that IV." She stated I had TENS, which is Toxic Epidermal Necrosis Syndrome. I had been diagnosed with something I had never heard of. She said most doctors have heard of Stevens Johnson Syndrome, but this is the most severe case of SJS.

This is a severe skin reaction to drug therapy, in which the skin disease results in eruptions resembling burns. It is often heralded by fever, sore throat, cough, and burning eyes. All of these symptoms, I had. The skin usually begins with a rash that later develops into blisters. I had blisters in my eyes, mouth, down my throat, in my respiratory system, torso, legs, arms, and in the GI tract. What happens is layers of your skin begin to detach from one another and in time the entire surface of the skin may be involved with detachment of one hundred percent of the epidermis. The drugs that most commonly cause TENS include antibiotics such as aminopenicillins, cephalosporins, and anticonvulsants. TENS is extremely rare, and I had it. Apparently, people with TENS seem to have difficulty metabolizing the medication. Some researchers suggest that certain substances that should be cleared from the body instead get deposited on the outer shell of the epidermis, causing an immune response that leads the body to "reject" the skin. Patients like me were typically treated in an intensive care unit or in a burn unit and receive treatment like what is given to patients with major burns.

I was very angry at this point. I told the doctors and the nurses that the antibiotic was causing my illness. Why didn't they listen to me? If it wasn't for the doctor from California, I would be gone. She saved my life. Now, I lay in a bed and may not ever recover. I was in excruciating pain and even the morphine wasn't helping not even easing the pain.

Have you ever been in a situation of which your life hangs in the balance? You're not sure how to manage, how to cope. Now I have a diagnosis, things had to get better, right? Well this is just the beginning of my story. Little did I know, my road was going to get a lot harder, more painful, and more heartbreaking, but on this road I get a lot stronger.

Wendi Landis-Talkington

HOSPITAL SEARCH

Now the search was on to find a hospital that could handle my condition. They called several locations but decided that Bronson's Burn Unit in Kalamazoo, Michigan, would be the best place for me to go. They put me in an ambulance and away I went, non-stop with sirens blaring. A good hour and half ride took about forty-five to fifty minutes to get there. I remember hanging on to the side of the bed trying not to move because my skin would come off whenever I would jostle. By the end of my ride, my skin was unbelievable painful. You see, our skin is covered in nerves, you know the feeling of a paper cut, well that's the only way to describe the painful sensation I felt all over my body.

As soon as I arrived at Bronson's, there was a team waiting for me. I kept thinking, how can this be happening to me? What did I do to deserve this? The blisters have continued to spread all over my body. I had large blisters everywhere and now some had grown the length of my arm.

I was treated like a burn victim, a topical antiseptic was placed on my blisters and wrapped me up like a mummy. You could see my nose and lips, but both were completely black like dying burnt skin. My skin was starting to necrose but the bandages made me feel comfortable. They were cool and wet with the antiseptic that felt soothing to my skin which was a reprieve.

I had never been seriously ill before, a cold or the flu from time to time, but I was healthy and now suddenly, I was fighting for my life.

What I am about to describe to you is graphic. It was part of my daily treatments meant to heal but was torture.

Every morning they would take me down to this bathing tank and they would strip the Necrotic skin from my body then place me in a saline bath. It was the worse pain I have ever felt. I remember begging them to skip the baths. I was normally a strong person, I didn't complain of pain before this all started, but this pain was so unbearable, my screams could be heard down the hall where my family waited. To this day my daughter can still hear my screams. It still torments them. Most days I would pass out from the horrendous pain. I understand this was part of the healing process and they were trying to save my life, but this was torture. Why? Why has God been punishing me and my loved ones? I did pray that something would happen, but this seemed cruel. My faith was slipping but my fight to live remained un-wavered. Unfortunately, my condition continued to worsen.

They decided it was time to place a central venous access catheter to keep track of my vitals and provide medications and fluids. This is a procedure that needs to be done in surgery because of the placement of the catheter. Before I had been completely bed ridden, I had pushed the button for help to go to the bathroom, the nurse wasn't coming and being an impatient person and very independent, I decided that I was going to go by myself. I got up off the bed and headed to the bathroom and suddenly, I couldn't move. Something was holding me back. I could see the bathroom, but I could not get to it. I stood there in my room and kept tugging and tugging trying to get to the bathroom and finally I was free from what was keeping me from moving. I made it to the bathroom and back to my bed successfully. The nurse finally came in to help me and I told her I had gone to the bathroom by myself. She stressed the importance of me waiting to be helped. She then looked down to the floor and said where is this water coming from? She then realized that I had pulled out my catheter to the heart. Well that wasn't good news. Little did I know I had already had the surgery, so back to surgery I went. This time when I came out of surgery, I came out with a urine catheter as well. So, I was now bedridden and since my body was so sensitive, my mattress was changed to an air bed. It was soft and gave a little reprieve from the pain. This helped to protect the skin

Wendi Landis-Talkington

from sluffing off. However, because the pain continued to progress, I got to the point that I was given medication to help repress the memory of pain from my mind.

THE POINT OF NO RETURN

When I first arrived at Bronson's my family asked me if I wanted to see the children and I said no. I knew that my chances for surviving were not good, and I wanted them to remember me as I was and not as I lay. My oldest daughter, Megan, was sixteen and was adamant about visiting, so I agreed that she could come up with her grandparents or her father to visit. My parents, family, and friends waited and prayed. I knew my parents were really having a hard time, especially my father. I was daddy's little girl. He always supported me no matter what. He never judged me, if I made a mistake, he never said, I told you so. I remember my father would stand at my bedside and try to lift my spirits. On one occasion, my toes were exposed, and he insisted on trimming my toenails. I told him it wasn't that important, and he argued until he got his way.

My organs were being attacked by TENS, and I was slowly slipping away. I don't know if you or someone you know has ever been in a critical care unit, but if you haven't, it is a very sad place to be. This is a place where some people pass away. It's an awful place for a family to sit and wait to see if their loved one will make it through the night. You hear familes cry out in sadness for their loved one. You hear people screaming in pain and screams when people lose their loved ones.

This is probably the most difficult to write about because I think of the pain that my family, friends, and children were going through. My daughter, Megan, was so young, she should not have to bare the pain of losing someone so close to her. It breaks my heart to think of the horror she was going through. Not only did she sit there and pray for me, but she heard my cries and the cries of families losing their loved ones. Was it the right decision for her to come to visit? I didn't know. I guess if it was me at that age, I would have demanded to be there for either one of my parents as well. I can't wipe out any of those moments for her or anyone else that was there during that time or for my other children at home not knowing what was going on with their mother. At that point in time, I knew I was fighting for survival.

A VISION

As I discussed early on, the ICU was a critical care unit, so people were fighting for life. My family received a call telling them it was urgent to come to the hospital. I was not doing very well, and I might not make it through the night. They all were overwhelmed with emotions. Unfortunately, this call was made on three occasions, so they were sure the third call would be the last.

I really don't remember anything about when they were called, but I do remember the experiences that made me feel very blessed. As I lay there, I remember hearing a voice of a dear friend who had recently passed from cancer. I heard her voice telling me that I needed to fight, and I told her I was trying. I was weak, I was in pain, and I was giving up. What I believe was the last time my family was called, I remember it like it was yesterday, my husband sitting at my bedside begging me not to leave him and the children. I heard the sniffles of my family wiping their noses and the cries of the family in the room. As I lay in that bed, I knew it was my time to go. I had decided that I had enough. I loved my family, but I was losing the battle. I said to my heavenly father in a voice of tears to let me go, I had no more strength to fight. I just couldn't do it anymore. I was tired, and I just couldn't take the pain. I begged for him to take me! Almost immediately, as I laid there on the bed, I felt total peace come over me. I felt someone touching my right shoulder. I looked over and saw a hand with the purest white sleeve and a perfect hand. I heard the voice of my Heavenly Father. In a soft sweet loving voice, He said that "it is not your time to go." As I looked up from my bed, I saw angels flying over me so fast like they were bringing life and strength back into my body and soul. They were giving me the strength that I needed to fight to survive.

At that point, I knew I had to fight, life was not over for me and I had to do whatever I needed to do to pull through. I knew at that moment there was a God and He was not letting me go. My prayer was answered; there is a God and he is with everyone. He made it clear that it was not my time to go. Every day that I laid in the critical care unit, I felt like someone was standing over me. The feeling was so strong, I kept looking behind me to see if someone was standing there. I finally came to realize that was my guarding angel watching over me.

I had received prayers from all over the world and I was on prayer chains in California, Utah, Japan, Europe, Australia, you name it, and the prayers were coming in from all over. I received letters and cards from people all over the United States. I am a firm believer in the power of prayer and I am most definitely a believer in God. I believe that every one of us has a purpose in life and we are here to stay until it is fulfilled.

ON THE ROAD TO RECOVERY

Due to the Necrotic skin I had a few skin grafts. That's where they take skin from a healthy area and place it on a dead area in hopes to generate new skin. Lucky for me, it worked.

As the days passed, the bandages started coming off. I lost my eyelashes, eye brows, and most of my hair from the illness. I had several doctors that would come in and check on me as I recovered.

With all the good news, I also received some bad news. TENS had attacked my liver. My liver numbers were not good. I had to have a liver biopsy to see how severe the damage was to the liver. I don't know if you have had a liver biopsy, but they make it sound like it is no big deal but let me tell you, it is not fun. The doctors tell you they will give you a little medication to make you comfortable and then they take you down to a procedure room and you lay on your side. They give you the medication in your IV to relax you and they numb the area with some Novocain. They take this sharp tube and put it in on your side up on your rib cage and then they shoot this claw like tool into your liver. They tell you not to breath, then the claw grabs the liver and then pulls a piece of it out. I doubt that any of the doctors that did this procedure to me had ever had it done or they might have been a little bit more honest about the procedure. At this point, my doctor felt that I might need a liver transplant. He said that sometimes a liver can rejuvenate on its own, if it isn't severely damaged. So that was our hope, that it would heal itself and no transplant would be needed. I, of course, was ready to go home. If we could give the liver some time to see if it would heal, I was all for that.

I went through therapy every day to try to get my legs and arms working again. I had a walker to help assist me in getting around. I went from 118 pounds to 98 pounds, so I was quite weak. Even brushing my teeth was a challenge when you don't have any strength. The therapist told me I would leave with a walker, but that was not in my game plan. At this point, I needed to show strength to the children, show them that I was the same person I was a before all of this happened. I knew life would not be the same, but I wanted everything to be as normal as it could be. Weakness was not an option, and I was determined to gain my strength back and go home without any assistance, so I walked. I walked the halls four to five times a day and sure enough before too long I was walking without a walker. I think we as people decide what our limits are. I think with a positive attitude and with determination, we can do anything we set our minds to.

I had a great staff of nurses and doctors at Bronson's. They took really good care of me and they treated me like I was a real person, like family. Sometimes hospitals and doctors forget that you have feelings and seem cold hearted. I am sure you know what I mean, we have all had them. Then you get one that you can talk to, that listens and does care. Those are the doctors and nurses that make the difference in peoples lives. I became close with one of my nurses. It turned out he also raised goats, and he wanted to give me a goat to take home. He said goat milk was good for me. Such a thoughtful nurse, but I lived in a city, so I could not take a goat home, but it was so thoughtful that he offered such a great gift.

Often, I would have nurses that would peak their head in the door that had taken care of me when I first arrived at Bronson's. They had not seen me since my bandages had been removed and wanted to see what I looked like. They would stop in and chat and say that I was a miracle patient and that I looked good for what my body had gone through. I told them that it was the power of prayer and the blessing of the Lord, that's why I am here today.

VISITORS

Since the hospital was about an hour and half away from home, I hadn't had many visitors. However, I did have a couple of bosses that I worked with, and they decided they were going to brave a snow storm to come up to visit. They asked if they could bring me anything, and without hesitation I said a Big Mac. Anybody who knows me knows I love food and boy did I want a Big Mac. I was tired of hospital food and I wanted to eat. It took me about an hour to eat that Big Mac, but I did it!

I also had some girlfriends that came up to visit. They tried to make me feel better by helping me do my hair and prepare for the visit of my children. In the beginning, before all of this happened, I had long brown hair. Unfortunately, it had been put in a rubber band to keep my hair away from my face since I entered the hospital. As my friends worked on my hair, I could see the looks on their faces and I knew my hair was coming out by the handful. Finally, I asked my husband just to cut out the rubber band. I knew with all the trauma I had been through, I figured my hair wasn't that important and would eventually grow back.

REUNION TIME

I asked to see my children. It was a few weeks before Christmas, and I really missed them. One Sunday afternoon, my parents brought them up to see me. It was a day for me to rejoice. I was so excited I could hardly stand it. When I saw their little faces peak their heads in my room, all I could do was cry. I was so thankful to finally be able to see and hold them. They were a little standoffish at first, since I did not look the same. I had a yellowish hue from the liver not working so well and I had several machines still attached to me, so it took them a few minutes to realize I may have looked different, but I was still the same person. After some coaxing, they finally sat on my bed and the hugs and kisses started to flow. I came to realize that sometimes life is so busy that I had forgotten how important those hugs are and the words, I love you, and from that day forward I would always make sure that I hugged and kissed them no matter how old they were.

They were all anxious to know when mommy was coming home and so was I. I told them the doctor gave me a goal of December 16th and I was determined to make that date.

HOMECOMING

December 16th was the day! I was so excited to be leaving the hospital. I did have concerns about how well I would do at home and I knew I had a long road ahead of me with lots of doctor appointments and follow-up care. I knew I would be traveling back and forth to Kalamazoo to the internal medicine doctor and I knew this was going to be an ongoing issue for quite some time. I was just so happy to be going home and I had come so far, I knew I could get through any of the obstacles I had to face.

I rode down in a wheel chair and I walked out the door without a walker. My determination paid off. My children would not see me with a walker, they would see me more like the person I was before all of this happened.

I remember the ride home from the hospital like it was yesterday, the ground was covered with snow and it was deep. It seemed like it took forever to get home. When I arrived home, the house never looked so good.

My neighbor was there cleaning the house, and the dog was so excited to see me, he almost knocked me down when I walked through the door. The kids were so happy I was home, it felt like I had been gone forever even though it was a little over three weeks. The neighbor helped with the children while I was away. She cooked, cleaned, and helped with the laundry.

For some time, we were fortunate enough to have friends, family, church members, and the children's school helped prepare meals and drop them off to lend a helping hand. I think my mother had the hardest task and that was keeping up with all the laundry that six people created, and believe me there was a lot of it. My mother would wash, dry, and fold the clothes, and my father would come and pick the laundry up and take them back to my mom to clean. My dad came over daily and would vacuum and do my dishes. He would help me get the children around for school and help with them after school. He knew that I was still weak from all that I had gone through and even though I would tell him I can do it, he would say just go sit down, I am going to do this.

A CHRISTMAS WISH

My husband was trying to work to pay the bills, but we were really struggling with only one income. I did have health insurance from work so that helped with some of the medical bills but not with the daily living bills and those were adding up. I had a long road to recover and still having issues with my liver, not knowing what the future would bring, was a bit unsettling.

The Christmas tree was up, and the kids had been decorating it. Unfortunately, I hadn't done any shopping before I became ill so even though there were no presents under the tree, Christmas was going to be special this year.

We were fortunate enough to have wonderful support from our family and friends. My friend and her husband called a radio station and put me on the Wish List for Christmas. She told them my story and the radio station called me and put me on the air. They blessed our family with gift certificates to help us out for Christmas. We received donations from the Gold Wing Rider Association; my daughters' high school cheerleading team would buy for the Salvation Army every year but this year they decided to buy for our family; the Indiana State Troops provided to shop with a cop for the family; and a family that I had grown up with usually donated to a charity every year but picked our family to help this Christmas.

The community in Elkhart, Indiana, came together. We are so blessed to live in a community that cares about the people who live in it. I can not give enough thanks to all those people who gave and prayed for our family.

There are not enough words to express how grateful my family and I are to all those people that supported us.

Christmas with my family was a blessed time. I have never felt so lucky. This Christmas was different. You know how everyone usually gathers and socializes and they say good bye, well this time there were lots of tears of joy and you could feel everyone's love. You could feel the warm spirit was with everyone and we all were just grateful to be all together.

THE MENTAL TOLL

Everyone did what they could to help us financially which was amazing. My mother and father put a fundraiser together with some help from friends and family to raise money to help with expenses for me and my friend who had a terminal brain tumor. We were blessed with a good turn out which helped us out with the mounting medical bills.

When something like this happens to you, it doesn't only happen to you, it affects everyone around you. My family and children took the hardest toll. My parents of course almost lost their daughter. I was always daddy's little girl and for him it was devasting. I was the only girl with three older brothers, and I want to say that me becoming ill really pulled my brothers and I closer than ever. We had a great relationship before I became ill, but afterwards it was more like really appreciating the love we had for each other and realizing how short life can be.

You know the parents are supposed to leave this life before their children, and being a mom, I can only imagine what my mother was going through. She always wanted what was best for me and would often voice her opinion but let me do what I wanted. She was always there when I needed her. My parents went above and beyond for me and supported me through this troubling time.

I was emotionally drained. I was on a mental roller coaster. I would cry over everything. I was just so thankful to be alive but so worried about what the future would hold, not knowing what medical issues the future would bring. With that being said, I had to do something that I thought only older people did and that was make a living will. That was very difficult for me to do. I was thirty-five years old and making a will. This was the last thing I ever thought I needed to do. I guess it should be done early on in life, but it's just one of those things you put off until you get older. I had to make choices about my quality of life and at what point to tell people to stop keeping me alive. I had to figure out who would be responsible for my children and I had to select a power of attorney. This was all so crazy for me. I had always been so healthy and now realizing that I might not be able to see my children grow up.

My children didn't know how to communicate their feelings or how to comprehend what took place or what was going to happen in the future. They all dealt with the trauma differently.

Megan, who was the oldest, really did not talk about it too much for the longest time. She is like me in the fact we tend to hold our emotions in and try to be strong for everyone else. Sometimes she would have a breakdown and cry but the more we talked about what happened the better she got. I know she will never forget and will deal with the memories of what she saw and heard, because I was her mom and the thought of almost losing me was very difficult to deal with. She was a cheerleader at the local high school and I was a JV cheerleading coach at the high school. We spent a lot of time together before all of this happened, so now suddenly, her mom was not there to participate in the activities. This was a big change for her, but with the support of her grandparents and friends, she became more confident that all would be okay.

Chelsea was ten at this time and became my shadow. She was having a hard time in school. Her teacher was very supportive as were all the teachers and principal at her elementary school. This was very helpful since they would encourage her to talk about her feelings and reassure her that she had lots of support and everything would be okay. She was like a little mother to me. She wanted to know where I was going, when I would be back, and if she could go. She was angry with me because when I fell sick, I went to the hospital and did not say good bye. I told her I would be back and then I didn't come back, so she felt angry since I was gone for such a long time. Most of the time, I would take her wherever I went to try and get her to feel more confident that I was doing fine.

Kyle and Cody were six at the time and were lost. During the time that I was away, the boys were shifted from house to house and stayed with some people they did not know very well. They were really confused about everything. Of course, I was mom, I took care and provided for them and they never stayed anywhere other than home or at their grand-parent's house. They couldn't focus very well, and I ended up holding them back to repeat kindergarten, so they wouldn't have to struggle so much in first grade. They had enough worries going on without having to struggle in school.

Never did I ever think that this could happen to me. It happened so fast with no time to prepare. I guess in life we don't always have time to prepare and the way we handle what happens to us either makes us stronger or it can break us. I was not going to let this defeat me.

I tried my best to keep an upbeat positive attitude, even though I had no clue on what the future would hold. I felt if I had the positive attitude that I was doing better, it would help my children get past the sudden ill-ness that nearly took me.

I heard lots of I love yous and received lots of hugs and kisses from all my children. My oldest who wouldn't be caught kissing me in public, kissed me openly in front of her friends and always said I love you. I didn't think I could ever hear those words enough. I am closer with all my chil-dren and family, including my brothers and sisters-in-law, now more than ever. It is a shame how you can live so close as family but forget to pick up the phone or send a friendly text, just to say hello and I love you and ask them about their day. It is too bad that it takes something so horrible to bring a family closer together. Unfortunately, it just seems like we really don't appreciate what we have in life until something tragic happens.

TRYING TO
BE NORMAL

I tried to get life back to normal for the sake of everyone. Unfortunately, my liver was not cooperating too well. I had another biopsy and there was no change and my liver numbers were not getting any better. By January, I had signs of a failing liver. My skin was jaundice. I was as orange as a basketball and I itched terribly. I was recommended at that time to go the University of Michigan in Ann Arbor for a possible liver transplant.

I made my first trip in January to U of M Hospital and they took seventeen vials of blood. I didn't think they were ever going to stop drawing my blood. The doctors reviewed my case and scheduled some additional tests to make sure the heart was not affected. The doctors explained that the liver is the only organ that can rejuvenate itself. It can heal on its own. The doctors felt there was a chance that the liver could recover and wanted to wait for a few months and see if the liver was improving before I would go on the United Network for Organ Sharing (UNOS) list. This is a list that your name goes on when a transplant is needed. A procedure that they can now do, other than using a cadaver liver, is take the right or left lobe of a liver from a person and put it into the person that needs a liver. The procedure is risky for both people and the donor must really know what they are getting into. That was something they talked about and something for me to consider but they were not sure that was an option for me.

I decided that it was important to take my children with me to the University of Michigan Hospital for my doctor's visits. I figure it was best to keep them in the loop, so they knew what was going on. I didn't want them to worry that I was going somewhere and not coming back. I felt I needed to gain their trust back. This way they would be able to ask questions and have them answered from the people who could explain it best. The doctor and the transplant coordinator were very friendly and made us all feel comfortable with what our next step could be. I told the doctor if I felt good, I wanted to go back to work. He agreed that I should work if that's what I wanted to do. I was meant to be here on earth, and I was not going to let this liver issue get me down.

In February 2001, I went back to work, and it was hard. I was so tired and still did not have much energy. I knew I needed to focus on something other than the liver and being sick. It felt good to be back in the work force and it gave me a sense of being normal. It also gave the children a sense of being normal with getting back into a routine again.

I continued taking trips to U of M and having my liver and kidney numbers checked. Sometimes when I would go to U of M, I would need to receive frozen red blood platelets. This was a cold process. They would wrap my arm in warm towels to help with the cramping of the cold blood going into the arm. This was uncomfortable and strange feeling but needed to be done. After several trips to U of M and a few more biopsies, I decided that it was time to stop working. I wasn't getting any better. My liver numbers were getting higher and I was growing weaker, so at the end of August of 2001, I decided it was time to stop working and focus on my health and the children.

BEING HOME

My children decided they loved me being home. I would get them off to school and I was home in the afternoon when they came home. I was able to go to their activities and bake cookies and have all kinds of time with them. Even though I grew weaker and more tired as time went on, I made sure that I didn't let out a whimper, so that no one would panic, especially my children. My dad would come over to check on me daily and see if there was anything I needed but I was insistent on doing the house chores myself. I also decided that I would get my Christmas shopping done early. I wanted to be prepared for whatever was ahead of me. I was not going to go through what I went through the year before, so this year I had all the Christmas presents wrapped and done in early October. Unfortunately, the only negative point was I forgotten what gifts I had bought. When you have liver problems as severe as me, your memory is not very good. My liver numbers were going sky high and it was obvious that it was not going to heal on its own. In late September, I was put on the list at U of M for transplant and the UNOS list.

CHANGE OF PLANS

After going to U of M, my liver numbers were over 1,000, when a normal number is 65. The liver can heal itself over time, but it was clear at this point, it was not going to do so. The doctors knew with a failing liver that my days were numbered. If I did not receive a transplant soon, I would die. The list I was on was very long, possibly a year wait or even longer.

I believe another angel came into my life at that point. With me being so young with small children there was concern that I would not be around to watch them grow up. I received an anonymous call in early October from someone telling me I could be multi-listed with other hospitals. This person gave me a few suggestions. I decided to call the University of Wisconsin and speak to someone there in the transplant office. I received a call back on a Thursday to come up to Wisconsin the following Tuesday to fill out paperwork and for an evaluation. We met with the surgeon, doctor, and transplant coordinator. The doctor looked at me and said I would be in the top three on their list because of my condition. It was my understanding that different hospitals have lists and depending on how sick you are with your liver numbers and the condition you are in, is where they place you on their transplant list. At least that's the way it was in 2001.

THE CALL

On October 23rd at 9:00 a.m. in the morning, I received a call from the clinic that they had a liver for me. I was overwhelmed with all kinds of emotion. I called my husband and my mother to tell them the news. My mother called the schools to let the kids know it was time to go to the hospital and the sitter was called for the boys. We had a friend from church that had offered to fly me to Wisconsin when it was time for the transplant. We contacted him and we met him at the airport. My daughters drove up with my parents to Madison, Wisconsin, where my transplant was going to take place.

We checked in about noon and the organ procurement team was on the way to retrieve the liver. Sometimes the liver that they retrieve doesn't work, sometimes they may find that it is damaged or that the blood type is not a good enough match for you, so you sit, wait, and pray that the liver is a good match. Otherwise you go home and wait for another day. About 6:00 p.m. we received word that the liver had been retrieved and it was a good match.

I don't know if you have ever been in a big hospital like this, but while you are waiting to hear if the liver is a match, you hear the helicopters take off and land. As I sat there, I felt saddened. The thought of someone dying, so that I could live, made me feel so overwhelmed with emotion. I felt very humble and grateful. I could only image the pain and suffering the family was going through just losing a loved one and then having the strength to donate their loved one's organs. They really didn't tell me much about the donor other than he was 41-year-old male and had been killed in a motorcycle accident in northern Wisconsin. They said they like to keep it private for the grieving family.

I wasn't sure if this was really happening, and it was happening so fast. Was I ready for this? What would life be like? Would this be permanent fix? As soon as they knew all was good with the incoming liver, everything just went quick. I went to a room on the transplant floor where they came in and took eighteen vials of blood and got me in my gown. They took me down to a holding room around 8:30 p.m. This is where they take you right before surgery and explain what is about to happen and what to expect in the recovery room and how long I would be in ICU. They explained to my family that I would have a breathing tube which would go down my throat to help me breath, I would be hooked up to too many monitors, I would have oxygen tube in my nose and that I would have several tubes coming from my body. I would have bags on my legs that would inflate and deflate on a timer to keep my circulation flowing. This helped prepare everyone, so they knew what to expect and that everyone goes through this process.

The doctors said the surgery would take several hours and not to panic. If it takes awhile to hear how things are going, that is usually a good sign and as soon as the surgeon had the liver out, he would come to the family and give them an update. Everyone was very kind and explained every step to the family. They started the IV and gave me something to take the nerves away. I remember looking over at my family and seeing the tears run down their faces and I reassured them that God has brought me this far, he is not letting me go now. I gave my hugs and kisses and away I went.

TRANSPLANT

They took me down the hall to the operating room. I remember being very cold. You know, I wasn't afraid, I figured if I could survive the burns that I had, that this would be a walk in the park. Once I was moved to the operating table, they had me count to ten and I don't think I made it to five and then I was asleep.

The surgeon had told the family that the surgery would take about eight to ten hours depending on how much blood was needed so prepare for a long night and try and get some rest. About five and a half hours went by and the surgeon came out and told my family it was over. My family was surprised! It was now 3:00 a.m. and it was over.

The surgeon said everything lined up perfectly just like it was my own liver. I only needed 1 unit of blood where some people require five units or more. The surgeon explained to my family that it was a miracle that I was alive because my liver was dead. It was gray and grainy. He said that someone was watching over me. He said I would be in ICU 48 to 72 hours depending on how I did and if there were any complications or rejections.

I was moved to the recovery room where I remember waking up and getting angry. I had the breathing tube down my throat and I wanted it out so I could talk. I motioned to my mother to get me a pencil so that I could write. I wrote down that I was fine, and I wanted to be off the respirator. You can't keep me down when I am raring to go! They took me off the respirator after twelve hours and the next tube to come out was the oxygen tube. I was in the ICU for forty-eight hours and then they moved me to the liver transplant floor.

RECOVERY

I was now on the transplant floor. It was amazing how much better I felt with a working liver. I felt perky and I was losing my yellowish orange glow. My eyes were finally starting to turn white. The nurses would check my wound from the transplant to make sure it was healing, and I was finally able to look down at my stomach to see what it looked like. The doctors called my scar a Mercedes Benz scar. It went from the bottom of my breast bone down to inches above my belly button and then down on each side of my stomach. I had fifty-seven staples in my stomach. I had four tubes inside my stomach around my liver area for drainage along with another tube that was attached to the bile bag. The bile bag collects the stuff that usually would go to your liver, and your liver would process it or filter it out. The bile bag was to help the liver not have to work too hard to help it heal before my body had to do it. The nurses or I would drain the bag when it would get full. One day a doctor came in and he told me it was time to pull two of the tubes from my stomach. I was thinking great I am on the road to recovery and this shouldn't be so bad. I asked the doctor if he was going to numb me before taking them out, but he said, "no, they just pull them out." Okay, this was not pleasant, and I thought I was going to go through the roof. They took the first one out and I asked them to wait on the second one and they said they had to pull two of them. It was a terrible cramping feeling and it was painful. After they pulled the tubes, they put a bandage over the holes and let them heal, no stitches needed. The problem with this was that I still had two tubes to go and I was not looking forward to the next two to be removed. I was still hooked to machines to monitor how I was doing, and they would draw my blood every morning to check my numbers. They had a huge chart on my wall and they would put all the liver and kidney numbers on the chart so when the doctors would come in they could see how my numbers were doing. They would check my vitals to make sure my blood pressure and temperature were also good to make sure I wasn't showing any signs of rejections.

Once I started to go through the transplant therapy and realizing what had happened and all I had been through, I really started to get angry. How could all of this happen from an antibiotic, why did my family doctor not listen to me in the beginning when I told him I was reacting to it? Why did he not try a different antibiotic? Why has he never called to see how I was doing? Even in the burn unit, he did not call. I still get angry about how my life has changed forever and there is nothing I can do about it except, accept it for what it is and try to move past it.

REJECTION

Everyday a group of about 10 doctors would come into my room to check on me. The University of Wisconsin is a teaching hospital, so the interns would come in and learn about my case. They drew my blood every morning to see if my numbers were getting better. They would drop a bit and then the next day they would go up. After the fifth day, my numbers were going back up and not flexing. I was in rejection, which means my body was not accepting the new liver. I called my mother and asked her to drive up because I was scared and lonely. I was about four and a half to five hours away from home so it wasn't easy for people to come and visit. My mother came up with my daughters to spend a few days and to give me support.

Now when your body starts to reject the liver, they have two kinds of serum they use to get your body to accept the liver. One of the serums was from a rabbit and one was from a horse, at least that's what it was when I had transplant in 2001. It is totally amazing what they can do with animals these days and how they can use them to help humans. These medications are so severe they warn you that you will feel like you have the flu for ten days after you receive it. They also warned of the side affects so they have a nurse sit with you for two hours checking your vitals every fifteen minutes. The nurse gave me some medication to help with the side effects of the serum. All went well for the first two hours and then it hit me. The nurse had just left because her two hours were up, and I started to get this ache pain in my back and then, suddenly, it felt like someone was standing on my chest. I had to stand up and my daughter went and got the nurse.

The nurse tried to get me back into my bed, but I couldn't breathe and sitting or lying down made it worse. The nurse paged for the doctor and they hit me hard with mediation to stop my reaction. The medication helped to relax my inner muscles, which were all knotting up. Within a few hours I was doing better, and I just felt crappy. Now this serum they gave me came in a series, so I had to get this for ten days but each time the reaction was better since my body was building up a tolerance to it. It did make me feel like I had the flu, but the serum worked. My numbers were finally coming down to where they needed to be.

TRANSPLANT FLOOR

As the days went on, I needed to exercise. I walked three times a day pushing my IV pole up and down the halls. As I walked down the halls, I noticed pictures of donors and recipients for kidney transplant patients. The kidney transplants were fast recovery patients. There were a lot of inner family donations for kidneys. You can live fine with one kidney if it is a good functioning kidney. Patients would come and go within a five to ten day period if everything was fine. It was amazing to see people come and go so fast for something so major. I also noticed a chart of the liver and the surrounding organs. After reading the chart, I realized they had removed my gall bladder and appendix. When I asked the surgeon about the chart, he said you don't need those organs and there is a chance they could cause problems down the road, so they might as well get rid of them to prevent this from happening.

The hospital performed all types of organ transplants. I was on the liver and kidney floor, but there was a lung and heart transplant floor as well. I was also surprised to see prisoners in handcuffs on my floor. There was an area for prisoners that had also had transplants. I guess I never really thought about prisoners getting sick and needing transplants, but they do. They were kept in a secured area with bars on the door and an officer that sat inside the secured area.

Sometimes while walking up and down the hallway, you would visit with people and hear their stories. One day I sat down and talked with a couple that came in because his wife needed a transplant and they received a call to come in. She said that there was a donor and they were going to split the liver with a three-year-old little girl. The little girl was going to get the left lobe and the woman was getting the right lobe. I was so amazed at the skills of these doctors and what they can do.

CLASSES AND MEDICATION

When you receive a transplant, you have daily classes that you must attend. These classes teach you what to expect with your transplant. You learn about all kinds of medication. You learn about each medication that you are taking and what the side affects are for each medication. They will bring your medication in with the wrong quantity or even the wrong type of mediation to see if you are paying attention to what you are taking. They tell you what medication you can take to help with some of the side effects of other medication. The anti-rejection medication I would be taking every day for the rest of my life. At this point, I was taking sixty-six pills a day and taking medication four times a day. It was crazy instead of eating, I would take a handful of pills and then I wasn't hungry. The cost of the medication was another big blow. One of my prescriptions was over $540 a month and I had several. How can people afford to live when their prescriptions are so high in cost? I was thankful for insurance. My main worry at that point was when would my insurance cap out. Since I had quit work, I was paying on Cobra which is extremely expensive.

You learn how to help your body heal and what to expect from your body. You learn how to know if you are rejecting your new organ and what to do if you show signs. You receive a little brown book where you document your weight, your blood pressure, and temperature daily. You find out how often you need to have your blood drawn and where all your liver and kidney numbers should be. You are given numbers to call for emergency and non-emergency calls. You are assigned a transplant coordinator and that person is your life line. At first, the blood draws were every couple of days and then every four days and that went on for months and then it went to one time a week, then every two weeks, then once every three and then once a month. After your draws you must phone your results in to the hospital on their hotline to make sure all your numbers are doing well. They also check the toxic level of your anti-rejection medication to make sure the level is not too high in your blood because that can damage your kidneys. You also learn that you now have a higher risk for thyroid and skin cancer and kidney issues because of the anti-rejection medication. You learn that you and all of your family members must get a flu shot every year. This must be done because your immune system is being suppressed and you are more susceptible to getting sick. After all of that, they encouraged you to live your life to the fullest and to be as normal as you want to be. Basically, everyone was sitting there thinking life will never by normal again.

LONELINESS

I was ready to go home. I only had a few more days of the serum left and then the doctor said I could go home. I had a wonderful nurse who took really good care of me. At one point I was extremely lonely. I missed Halloween with my children. I missed my son's ' birthday and I was getting depressed. My family lived about five hours away and I was in a room all by myself. I felt ache from the serum and I was feeling sorry for myself. I sat in the rocking chair with my knees pulled up to my chest in my room and cried. I felt crappy and alone. My nurse was very caring and gave me a hug and told me that life would be close to normal someday. She gave me comfort in her voice and in her hugs. She knew I was lonely, since my family lived so far away, she would visit me as often as she could.

I knew I had one tube that still needed to come out before I could go home, and I knew the other one would be there for a few months yet. I was dreading the tube coming out since it had been attached for about three weeks. I figured it was probably well attached. The nurse had come in and told me they would be pulling the last tube that night. I asked for a sleeping pill because I was extremely anxious just anticipating them coming in to remove it. The doctor came in early in the wee hours of the morning to pull the tube. I was well-sedated from the sleeping medicine. It seemed like I was dreaming. I remember not being very happy and yelling at the doctor because it felt like the tube had grown attached. When I woke up the next morning, I got up and washed up before breakfast, I looked down and noticed the tube was gone. What a relief! I was so thankful it was over. When the doctor came in the next day to check on me, I apologized. I told him, I thought I was dreaming because I had taken two sleeping pills and if I said something that wasn't nice, I was sorry. He just laughed at me and said he slid in around 3:00 a.m. and pulled it out. He said sometimes it is better to be a little sneaky, so it doesn't seem too bad. I asked if I could go home and they said I could on one condition, and that was to stay in Wisconsin for a week or two to make sure everything was okay. They didn't want me to go five hours away and then have an issue with the transplant.

OFF TO A HOTEL

I was admitted on October 23ʳᵈ, 2001, and now I was being released on November 14ᵗʰ, 2001. My mother and daughter Chelsea came up to take me to the hotel and to drive me back and forth to my clinic appointments. The hospital was great about making arrangements for the hospital patients. They arranged for us to stay a few miles away from the hospital with long stay rates. It was so nice to be with my daughter. They had a swimming pool and game room, so she had things to do which kept her mind from worrying about me. One night at the hotel I noticed my bile bag was leaking, and I was worried that I had accidentally pulled the tube away from my liver. There was fluid all over my bed. We went into the hospital emergency room in the middle of the night to have them check to make sure everything was okay. They had the on-call transplant doctor come in and check to make sure all was okay. I knew I was going to have the bile bag for at least ten to twelve weeks, so I didn't want to have another tube put in which would be a set back and keep me in Wisconsin even longer. Everything appeared to be fine. The doctor thought the bile bag was bad, so they replaced it. Thank goodness it wasn't more serious than that. Every other day I would go to the hospital to have blood drawn. I was free from direct hospital care, but I still wanted to go home. One morning while I was there, I received a phone call at the hotel, it was my daughter Megan. She was on her way to school and she was in an accident. She was scared and crying, but she was okay. My heart sunk to the floor. When you are sick and so far away from home you feel helpless. My children needed me at home and I was just too far away. I grew more aggravated about being there. I knew I had a check up at the clinic the following week and I was going to plead to go home. On November 21st I went to the clinic for my check up and I told them I wanted to go home. It was almost Thanksgiving and I wanted to be with my family. After quite a bit of hesitation, the doctor said okay, if I would promise if there were any changes of any sort I would come back to Wisconsin immediately, he would let me go home, so I promised.

My mother wanted to have the gentleman that brought me up to Wisconsin fly me home. I said, "No, let's drive! I can be home before the pilot would even get here." With my mother being very hesitant, she agreed to drive me, so away we went. The ride was rougher than I had anticipated, and I was extremely nauseated but there was no place like home and that's where I wanted to be. I called my children and told them I was on my way home and that I would see them soon! This was going to be a wonderful Thanksgiving this year!

HOME AND REST

I came home on a Tuesday and Thanksgiving was on Thursday. It was a time to be thankful. It was the best meal I had in a long time and I felt great. It is amazing how good you feel when your body is functioning as it should. The day after Thanksgiving, I went to have my blood drawn. My father was my chauffer. He would take me to the hospital for my lab work and bring me home. Blood draws were four times a week, then three times a week, then two times a week, then finally once a month. After I would get my blood drawn, we would go get some breakfast and discuss the plans for the day. As he did before, he would help me at home with dishes and vacuuming until I had my strength back. He would help grocery shop, pick up medication, and help me with the kids. My dad was always there to help me with whatever I needed. I was so blessed to have such great parents.

I still had the bile bag, so every day I had to clean my wound and apply new dressings. I had to empty the bile bag several times a day. As my numbers started to improve, my body started to function like it should and I was gaining strength every day.

Christmas was getting closer and the kids were all excited. I was home and we were getting into a normal routine again. This year I was prepared for Christmas since I had my shopping done in October. The presents were already wrapped and under the tree and Christmas would be as wonderful this year as it was last year. Some of the worries from last year were gone, since I had my transplant and I was doing so well. The children could be kids this year without having the worries they had the previous year. Finally, their worries were starting to fade. Before I knew it, it was New Year's.

I had plans with a new out look on life. You know the little things you take for granted like getting up every morning and just listening. I learned to hear the birds and listen to their song, look up at the sky like you used to when you were a kid and find the animals in the clouds. Look at the millions of stars that light the night, notice the sunrises and the sunsets. Smell the rain, the burning leaves, flowers that you walk by. The grills that are cooking in the summer time, the smell of fire places burning in the winter, the beauty of fresh fallen snow on the branches of the trees, breathe in that fresh winter air that is so clean and crisp. Have you ever listened to a train in the distance or an airplane as it flies over head, or the laugh of a child? Isn't it funny when a child laughs, you laugh. There are so many things that God has given to us and most of us don't take the time to stop and feel the goodness. God gave us eyes, a nose and ears, why do we not take the time to notice all the beauty around us? It doesn't matter if you are rich, poor, or middle class, all of these things are free and are around us every day. I urge everyone to take a minute of their day to notice the beauty around them. It really does wonders for your mind, body, and soul.

SIMPLE PROCEDURE

It was February now and it was time to have the bile bag removed. I was not looking forward to it. I knew how it felt to have the other tubes removed and this one had been in for sixteen weeks, so I knew it probably had grown attached. My mother and her girlfriend took me up to Wisconsin for the procedure. I went into the transplant clinic, which is attached to the hospital, and they prepped me for the procedure. The doctors said they would give me something to relax me through the IV and they would put a little camera down through the tube to the liver while they pull it out. In some cases, they said if they can't get it, they must do surgery to remove it immediately. I knew at that point, I would need to have surgery because for me nothing was simple. I am the person, if it can happen, it will. Sure, enough they were tugging, and the tube was stuck, so off to surgery I went. They made an incision on the right side where my scar was from the transplant to help minimize additional scaring. They removed the tube from the liver and stapled me back up. They gave me pain medication and kept me for a few hours and sent me to a hotel for the night. That night I was in so much pain that I went back to the hospital and they admitted me for a couple days until the pain was tolerable and then I was able to go home. Boy, was I glad that was over, and I didn't have to worry about the bile tube any longer.

A REBIRTH

On March 23rd, 2002, I got to go back to work. Finally, back to forty-hour work week and it felt great. Now I was feeling healthy and ready to get back to normal. As time passed, they started taking me off some of my medication. My body was doing well with the new liver. This was exciting and I was doing better every day!

Once my body started to heal, it went through a rebirthing process. After you have so much trauma, your body tends to begin over again. My hair began to grow; however, it was now gray but at least I had it. My eye lashes and eye brows grew back as well. Unfortunately, I had begun to have troubles with my eyes. When I was in the burn unit in Kalamazoo, I had a blister on my right eye. The doctors were watching the eye carefully because they thought eventually I might need a cornea transplant. The eye eventually healed from the blister, but when my eyelashes grew back, they grew into the eye instead of out towards the skin. So, in order to help solve this problem, I would go every four to six weeks to have them pulled. Since I had TENS and immune suppressed, I was susceptible to eye infections and eye problems. The membranes in my eyes have been burnt so my eyes are severely dry and irritated all the time and sensitive to light. I always wear my sun glasses even if it was cloudy to help with the sensitivity and prevent certain types of eye infections.

After several months of eye lash plucking, I was sent to an ophthalmic plastic surgeon to see if he could help with the way my eye lashes were growing. What they were going to try and do was to take a wire down to the root of the eyelash and burn it. Hopefully this would help them from growing back and into the eye. However, the lashes were not growing straight out because the eyes had been burnt and the eye lids were all scarred so it would be a trial and error process. It lasted for about three months and then more lashes would grow and then they would do the process over again.

My skin had some scarring, but I was lucky because it wasn't really that noticeable. I had little white bumps all over my face which I am still working hard to get rid of.

I would say that mentally, I was also going through a rebirthing process. I began to try and figure out my purpose in life. After all, I was saved by the hand of God. Why? I think everyone has a destiny in life, a purpose, something that needs to be accomplished before we begin our journey in the eternal life.

LIFE GOES ON

As I was dealing with my eye issues, which seemed minor compared to everything else I was dealing with, the regular daily activities and stresses were mounting.

My children were still suffering the affects of my trauma. The boys were struggling a bit in school and they were very small for their age. They didn't care for being small. I would always tell them that a lot of special gifts come in small packages. It doesn't matter how small or tall you are, it is what you do with yourself and how you treat others that count. Since they were so young, I think they were more trusting and when I said I was doing great, they were comfortable with what I said. Chelsea was still my shadow. When I would go back to Wisconsin for my yearly checkups, I would take turns taking the kids. This would give me some one on one time with them and bring them comfort knowing how well I was doing.

In 2003 my daughter Megan was gearing up for graduation. I remember her walking to the graduation march as I cried. I was able to see her grow and graduate. I wasn't sure what my future would hold but I was truly grateful to be sitting there and watching her in the moment! Her goal was to be a nurse. She took such great care of me, I knew she would make a great one.

In 2004, it was time for me to divorce my husband and head towards a more peaceful life. I prayed that God would give me the strength to get through the divorce. I knew that God had been there for me every step of the way and I could count on him now to get me through this. When you marry a man, you are also marrying his family. I loved his family deeply, but I couldn't stay married because of them. You see, I made a promise to myself that I would not spend the rest of my life fighting with my husband and the children needed stability. Enough was enough, no more arguments, no more yelling, I wasn't staying in a marriage where I was the mother and the father in the relationship. Life is just too short!

The children struggled for a while because their dad was not in a stable environment, but once everything calmed down the children were better. The boys would see a counselor to help them express their feelings, and frustration and they learned it was okay to be angry and that things would get better.

At that time, I should have been more insistent that all the children see a counselor. I did not force them to go, but I should have. Even though Megan was not living at home any longer and Chelsea was in high school, I think it would have benefited them and me as well.

TIME TO MOVE ON

As time went on, I kept praying for strength. I knew I had a tough road ahead of me, but I needed to do the best I could as a single parent. I made mistakes, but I kept trying to do better. Many times, I would float money so that I could buy groceries or pay bills, which bill could I put off, and which was most urgent to pay.

I would tend to err on the side of caution when it came to the children being sick. I wanted to make sure they were okay. I guess I was probably over protective, but I didn't know how not to be.

My parents were there to help along the way and help financially when they could, and that helped a lot. Megan had moved out on her own and was going to college part-time and working for the hospital. The boys, Chelsea, and I moved in with my parents for a while until I was able to purchase a home. Chelsea was on the cheer squad at the high school and Kyle was in the high school marching band. Cody was on the wrestling team and was the track manager. As a single parent, I tried to provide the best I could on one income. I bought a home at a twelve percent interest rate right before the economy crash in 2008. I tried to refinance, but the bank wouldn't lower the rate. My ex-husband wasn't paying child support on a regular basis and owed back support. At the time I bought the home, child support had been figured into my income which I wasn't getting, so eventually I lost my home. This was a very hard loss. This was stability for me and my children which was so important. I felt like a complete failure at this point in my life. Thankfully my parents let us move back in with them until I got my feet back on the ground.

Eventually we were able to move into an apartment across town which made me feel independent again. I wanted to be able to provide for my children because it was my job. My goal was for my children to do better in life than I had done. I wanted them to go for their dreams and get their college education. I did not want my children to go through life like I had. I did not want them to live pay check to pay check like I had been doing for years.

During our apartment days, I taught the boys how to drive and helped them with their drivers training class. I went to all the school activities that I could. I watched Megan graduate college, I watched Chelsea graduate and move on to cosmetology school, and watched and celebrated the boys' graduation.

AT THIS POINT AND TIME

Megan is now thirty-four years old. She has turned out to be an amazing young woman. She has been married for six years to Nicolas and has two children, Lainey who is five and Rex who is four. She is in nursing and teaches nurses and doctors how to put information into the software systems. Last year she was a surrogate for a couple and carried their twins. She is the most selfless person I know. I don't know how she did it. It takes a special person to be able to do what she did, and her husband was right by her side and supported her the whole way through. She gave a couple that couldn't have children the gift of life. It didn't matter what she was going to put herself through, it was always about what she could do to help someone else. Megan puts everyone else's needs before her own. She is such a strong and caring person. I admire her in so many ways.

My daughter Chelsea is now twenty-seven years old. She is married to AJ who is a farmer and they have two boys, William who is four and Jackson who is two. She has her cosmetology degree and still does some hair on the side, but she is a stay at home mom for now. She loves everybody and every animal on the planet. If she could save the world, she would. She doesn't like watching the news or the sad animal commercials, because it angers her. She doesn't understand why people do what they do. She has grown up to be a beautiful person inside and out and has a heart the size of the state of Texas. I admire her every day for having such a huge heart and being so caring. Her anxiety gets to her at times, but her husband is there to help her get through the tough moments. He is her rock.

I think all my children have anxiety, and I think it probably is my fault. They have been through so much, how could they not have anxiety? All I can tell them is one day at a time. I know it's easy for me to say but it is hard for anybody that has anxiety because they are stuck in the moment and it takes a while to push through it. I can only reassure them in time, you learn how deal with anxiety in a better way. You learn that what you can't control, you must let go and only worry about the things you can control.

Kyle is working on getting a degree in health information technology. He works part-time and goes to school part-time. We are looking forward to his graduation from college next spring. Kyle is very self-driven. He has goals and he is achieving them. He is very organized and self-motivated. He is very passionate in everything that he does. If there is something he believes in, he will fight for it. Some day I see him in politics because he believes in fighting for people's rights. He won't settle for second best, he wants to be the best in all that he does. I so admire the passion that he has and his drive. It will take him so far in life. I see such a bright future for him.

Cody was a police cadet for several years and took criminal justice classes at college. He is very independent and has been since high school. You can't tell Cody what he can't do because he will over come any challenge and prove you wrong. Cody has had to fight for all that he has achieved since he was young. He had a learning disability, but he didn't let that stop him from achieving his goals. He had a therapist tell him he would not be able to drive and would probably not graduate high school and more than likely would never live on his own. He proved that therapist wrong. He received his driver's license, graduated with a diploma, and has been enrolled in college classes. He lives on his own and is perfectly able to take care of himself. He is working as a Correctional Officer and is thankful for not giving up and kept pressing forward. I have always told him, you can achieve anything you set your mind to and he has. Some people would have given up and said I can't do it. Not Cody, he has consistently fought to achieve the things he wanted. Cody is a fighter! I so admire his inner strength!

UNEXPECTED
SADNESS

So far, I would have to say it's been a wild ride. There have been lots of ups and downs, struggles and victories along the way. Change is the only constant thing in my life, and at this point, my new normal.

On February 13th, 2017, at 11:47 p.m., I lost my father. This was devastating to me, my children, my brothers, my mom, and to all that knew him. He died unexpectedly that day, and it just shocked us all. I think at that moment, I realized that with life comes death. It wasn't possible that he was gone. As the family sat at his bedside and watched him take his last breath, it was just surreal. I was and still am in shock. How could this happen? Just a few hours before he was eating candy and graham crackers. He had fallen at home the day before and hit his head on the rocking chair. He was eighty-five years old and wasn't in the best of health, but he had all his wits. By the time I got to the ER, they had been doing some tests and he was alert and joking. They told us they were going to keep him overnight and give him an MRI in the morning. The VA hospital was trying to talk my father into getting a pacemaker and he wasn't so sure he wanted to get one. When I was with him in the ER, I was pressing the issue for him to get the pacemaker, he told me that everyone must go some time and I told him, I wasn't ready for him to go. He laughed and said okay. The next morning, he had an egg omelet and had some candy and graham crackers and they wheeled him down for his MRI. Less than ten minutes later he was back in the room complaining of a headache like he had never had. They couldn't do the MRI because of the amount of pain he was in. The neurologist came in and gave him something to relax him and that was the last I saw my dad awake. He had suffered a brain aneurysm and he had slipped into a coma. We had to make the decision to let him go or operate on him. If they saved him, he wouldn't be the same and they had no idea of the extent of the aneurysm. My dad had expressed many times, that if something would happen to him, let him go. He didn't want to live in a nursing home and if he wasn't able to care for himself, then he didn't want any intervention to keep him alive. With knowing his wishes, we as a family decided to let him go.

For some reason, I felt my dad would live forever and his passing was not an option. He was and always will be the love of my life. He was a great dad, husband, grandfather, brother, and friend. He was not only a father to me but my children as well. He taught them to ride bikes, tie shoes, swim, read, and do math. He helped me teach them manners and how to be respectful. He taught the boys how to build and fix things.

My children and I helped my parents out for many years. In my parents' older years, we helped maintain their home. We fixed things around the house, mowed, shoveled, maintain the pool, raked the leaves, prepared meals, and ran errands for them. We tried to take care of them and return the help they gave me over the years.

Life would never be the same without my dad and trying to figure out how to live without him was going to be difficult for all of us.

MY JOURNEY FORWARD

It has now been 18 years since transplant, and I am almost fifty-four years old. A lot has happened over the past eighteen years. My children have all grown up, I have grandchildren, and I have dealt with death.

God has given me so much over the past several years of my life. I have been blessed to see all my children graduate from high school, watch my daughters get married, able to see the birth of my grandchildren, and watch them start kindergarten and preschool. I have been able to watch my children grow up to be amazing adults and I am so proud of each of them.

My health is great! When I first started this journey, I asked the doctors what my life expectancy would be, and they said it depended on how good the liver match was and how well I took care of myself.

I have been doing well except for the eyes. My eyes get irritated easily. They are sensitive to makeup, chemical, odors, and the constant lash irritation. Unfortunately, the doctor said no more surgeries, so I will continue to get the lashes pulled until the end of my days and just deal with it.

I am doing well with medication. I take a blood pressure pill, multivitamin, magnesium, vitamin C, daily aspirin, vitamin D with calcium, and my anti-rejection medication, Tacrolimus. I went from sixty-six pills a day to just a few. I have had a great recovery. The anti-rejection medication is at a low dose. Last year at my transplant visit, we talked about weening me from them. There is a chance if they reduce it, I could go into rejection. My doctor said it's up to me. If I stay on the medication, I have a higher risk of some cancers and kidney issues, but there are people who have been successful with getting off the medication. It's a future decision I must make and risks either way.

The medical costs mount up every year. I do have medical insurance, but with the high deductibles increasing, medical bills just put us in debt every year. You try to save for retirement, but it's difficult to do when you have such high medical costs.

NEW CHAPTER

On July 12, 2014, I began a new chapter in my life. I married a wonderful man who takes such good care of me. He was my friend and ended up being my husband and soul mate. Maybe God's plan in the beginning was for me to go through the rough times in order to find the right person in life. If life hadn't played out the way it had, I wouldn't have found the husband I have today.

I am very lucky that my dad got to meet him and spent some time with him. My husband is a very tall man and my father was always amazed that he could change a lightbulb in the ceiling without ever using a ladder. After my father passed, my husband agreed to bring my mother into our home. He felt she wasn't in the best of health to live on her own, so we bought a house and we converted the basement to an apartment for her. This way she could still have her own place, but we would be here if she needed anything.

I warned him when he proposed that he didn't want to marry me because my life was so unpredictable that I didn't know what was around the corner. My life was chaos most of the time. I am not a normal person, I couldn't promise stability because my life was so unpredictable. I warned him that I was a crazy lady and I had nothing to offer other than love and laughter. He said if he wasn't sure he wouldn't propose and he could handle anything that I could throw at him. He has met every challenge that has been thrown his way. I can't image one day, one minute, or even one second without him in my life. He has been there to help me through moments of chaos, anxiety, and my father's passing. Just hearing his voice is enough to calm me, when I am upset or having moments of anxiety. I believe that God has a hand in everything, and he brought me Sean!

PURPOSE

What is my purpose in life? I believe I was meant to be here for my children. I think if I hadn't survived, their lives would have been turned upside down. I am not the perfect parent and never have been. I have made many mistakes along the way. I believe I am here to support them and do whatever I can to help them.

A lesson I have learned along the way, words are like daggers, once you get stuck with one, you will always have a scar. I have said things that I wish I hadn't said. I think it is a reflex, someone says something to you that is hurtful, and we strike back quickly and then more times than not, we regret the words that we have spoken.

My father taught me that you can solve most problems by talking your way through it. I do carry on conversations out loud instead of in my head. Does that make me crazy? My husband thinks it's hilarious. Sometimes he says I carry on part of a conversation in my head and then finish it out loud. I find it funny that he can figure out what I am trying to say or want to do without hearing the whole conversation. I am very thankful to have found someone that understands me.

I think without a doubt that I have become a stronger person after all that I have gone through. Many challenges have been thrown my way, and I have learned to deal with them. Maybe God's plan, was for me to find my inner strengths and to learn by having faith, I can get through my darkest times. In the beginning of my book, I questioned, how do I know that there is a God? And my question was answered.

Every day is a new day and a day I feel blessed. I am a miracle, someone that shouldn't be here today. I believe in God with all my heart, mind, and soul. I believe in the power of prayer. I thank God for families who are donors. If it wasn't for a donor, I wouldn't be here today. I believe that we all have a guardian angel that stands beside us each and every day. I hope that all of you readers have felt a warm spirt as you have read my story and I hope that if you had any doubts about our Heavenly Father, that your doubts have been washed away. I hope that you all take the time to say I love you to your family and friends. I hope that you all take the time to notice the gifts that God has given us. Take time to stop and listen, smell, and feel his goodness. Please take time to thank God for his goodness and his love. May you all receive wonderful blessings in your life, like I have in mine.

Whatever life throws at you, don't let it define you! Live life to its fullest, live life for each day, and don't worry about tomorrow.

THE END